All About
ROULETTE

John Gollehon

D0827813

A PERIGEE BOOK

Perigee Books
are published by
The Berkley Publishing Group
200 Madison Avenue
New York, NY 10016

First Perigee Edition 1988

Photo credit: The front cover features a striking photograph of the original roulette wheel used when the Desert Inn first opened in Las Vegas in 1950.

Unlike the wheels used today, this particular device was all hand-built with inlaid hardwoods, and nested in a hand-carved wheelhead showing a motif of a Western landscape.

The wheel itself weighs over 100 pounds, and even today is pressed into service on busy weekends at the Desert Inn.

ISBN 0-399-51460-0

Printed in the United States of America
10   11   12   13   14   15

CONTENTS

CHAPTER 1

CAN ROULETTE BE BEATEN?

Of all the games and devices in the casino, the one that most identifies gambling is the roulette wheel. Remember the movie *Casablanca*, and Humphrey Bogart's famous scene at Rick's cafe? Whenever a movie or television producer wants to be sure his audience understands that a scene takes place in a casino, he first shoots a close-up of the spinning roulette wheel. As if to say, "Look, we're in a casino. See, there's the roulette wheel!" Even if the filming is on a sound-stage on the back lot at Universal, the roulette wheel has to be there to *make* it a casino. In the world of make-believe, roulette exemplifies gambling.

But what about the real-world? Studies have shown that people who have never been in a casino expect to see roulette wheels all over the place. I suppose you could blame the movie producers.

Based on these same studies, if you ask the people to name the casino game that first comes to mind, it's . . . you guessed it, roulette.

It's the strangest paradox. Those of us who frequent casinos know that there are few roulette tables compared to the other games. A typical casino layout might include 30 blackjack tables, six craps tables, two baccarat tables, and one or two roulette wheels. Depending on the time of day, it's possible that the roulette dealer might just be standing around picking his nose. No players. No action.

According to a 1984 "Visitors Profile" commissioned by the Las Vegas Convention and Visitors Authority, less than 2% of all visitors to Las Vegas play roulette. From that same study, we can determine that 45% play blackjack, 30% play slots, and 8% play craps. Even more players try their luck at the new video poker machines, in fact, five times as many! Maybe what this game needs is *video* roulette!

When you realize that one out of every two visitors to Las Vegas play blackjack, you have to wonder why roulette seems to get all the glory. Blackjack is indeed the most popular casino game, and for a host of reasons. And we all know how popular slot machines are. Over 50% of the casino's gaming revenue comes from slot machines. And some casinos have over 2,000 machines!

I know, this book is about roulette, not slots or blackjack. But an understanding of how roulette compares to the other games is vastly important. And equally important to our discussion of roulette is learning why the game appears to be on the down-side. Roulette is indeed losing its appeal.

The next few pages will delve into this interesting contradiction, an important step before we learn the basic rules and percentages. I respectfully ask that you do not simply skip to the next chapter, looking for the "meat" of this book. The "meat" might very well be in the next few pages. Incidentally, if you do elect to skip the rest of this chapter, the book will self-destruct in ten seconds.

A BRIEF HISTORY LESSON

It's always fun to find out how a game originated. I suppose I could tell you that roulette was invented in Nome, Alaska by two Eskimos on a cold July day in 1897, on the theory that they had absolutely nothing else to do. Many of you will probably believe that.

No? OK, how about a Frenchman in 1657? Sound better? Indeed, France gets the credit for roulette like so many other casino games. But to be perfectly frank (no pun intended), most readers couldn't care less when and where the game originated. The big concern is beating the damn thing today!

None the less, a little history lesson right now can't hurt us, and might very well key an important fact that will help us beat the game.

Roulette has remained essentially unchanged in its concept since its European "modernization" over 200 years ago. Although the "Americanized" version sports an extra "0" (green spot), the game has stood the test of countless mathematicians, gamblers, and cheaters over the centuries to such a degree that something has to be learned from all this; indeed, somewhere in the writings, articles, papers, books, and essays there has to be some interesting twist that we can use today. And there is.

THE MATHEMATICAL ASSAULT

Roulette is an easy game to determine mathematically. Although this isn't the right time to study the wheel in mathematical terms (see chapter 2), it's important to realize from the outset that mathematically, it can't be beaten over the long term. In other words, "luck" isn't going to make it.

If we consider the wheel a symmetrically perfect device, able to produce purely random numbers, we might as well stop right now. Roulette has a built-in mathematical advantage for the house that simply won't budge. Your mathematical assault means "with luck," and if that's the best you can do and as far as you want to take it, I suggest you return this book to where you bought it. Let the salesperson read this paragraph, then boldy ask for your money back! If you can't get it, threaten to sue, or call your attorney.

Like I said, a study of all the possible outcomes, odds, and probabilities of roulette will lead you to a chilling mathematical conclusion. The game ain't fair!

Luck is Where You Find It

The sheer mention of "luck" as a force against a casino game always brings to mind a funny incident that happened in Las Vegas at the Desert Inn. For those of you who are not familiar with the Desert Inn, let me tell you that the casino is one of the finest anywhere, relatively small and intimate, situated to the right of the hotel as you walk in at the main entrance. Straight ahead of the entrance, and to the left (directly beside the bar) is a restroom, strategically located. For most of us, with all the drinks available in the casino, that particular restroom becomes a popular pit-stop.

One evening, I entered the restroom and walked to the back where there are three urinals (trust me). There was a guy using one of them, and two were open. Another guy was just standing there, as if waiting his turn. I walked up, reviewed the situation, and ask this guy, "Excuse me, are you waiting or what?" He said, "Yea, go ahead, I have to use this one (pointing to the urinal on the right, being used)." I had to ask him why, right? He said, "It's my lucky urinal! Before I play, I always come in here and . . . ."

Good gosh! This jerk doesn't have a lucky coin, a lucky shirt, or a rabbit's foot. No. Not *this* guy. He has his own lucky urinal!

I suppose if you're playing at the Desert Inn, and things just aren't going your way . . . well, remember, it's the stall on the right.

THE "SYSTEMS" ASSAULT

Along the same lines as trying to beat the wheel with luck—that we called the "mathematical" assault, is perhaps the most time-tested of them all . . . *systems*. Since day-one, even the most astute mathematicians have tried countless, esoteric systems of picking the numbers or making the wagers. None of them have ever worked. None of them ever will.

There are several systems widely popularized based on picking the number, color, or odd/even factor that is based strictly on previous numbers. Keeping track of the wheel's decisions with pencil and paper is a complete waste of time. It should be elementary, but needs to be said . . . **the wheel has no memory**. Previous numbers have no effect on future outcomes.

If red has come up five times in a row, the next spin will yield no more or no less a chance for red to come up again, regardless of the scoreboard. The odds are the same every time the little white ball drops. This, my friend, you must believe.

Since there are 38 compartments on the American "Double Zero" wheel—18 red, 18 black, and two green—the odds are easy to compute. There are 38 probabilities all total. And we know there are 18 ways to make red. So, the correct odds of winning on red are 10 to 9. Here's how we get it.

The first number in an odds expression represents the number of times an event will *not* happen. The second number in the expression represents the number of times it will. The total of both numbers in the correct odds expression is the total number of all probabilities, win or lose.

If there are 38 probabilities total, and we know that there are 18 probabilities that will win, the difference is obviously the number of probabilities that will lose—20. So, the odds are 20 to 18, reduced to 10 to 9. Expressed as a percentage against you it's 1/19 (one net loss out of 19 trials) or 5.26%.

Similarly, the many systems being touted that deal with betting progressions are equally useless and deserve little space here. It's important that you realize that no method of varying your bets will change the expectancy. It makes absolutely no difference, *over the long term*, how you vary your bet size. If you wish to challenge me on that statement, go play. At some point in time, the wheel will have taken every cent you have.

Now we know all the ways that you can't beat a roulette wheel. You can't beat it mathematically. Luck is no factor. Tracking the numbers is a sucker's system. And foolish betting progressions are for losers.

I purposely put the two "losing" assaults first, and left the best for last. Now, let's look at two assaults that seem to make sense, and might have some merit.

THE "WHEEL BIAS" ASSAULT

The idea of a roulette wheel having some sort of bias is not new, but represents the basis for some new, interesting theories.

Over the years, gaming authors have contended that a roulette wheel cannot be perfectly symmetrical, cannot be in perfect balance, and cannot have precisely the same compartments. Technically, it has to be true. Nothing in this world is perfect . . . except my mother-in-law.

The roulette wheel is indeed precision-machined and constructed. Every effort is made to insure a random distribution of numbers by eliminating any potential bias. But there are so many wheels in operation; can they all be perfect? Isn't it possible that at least a few are defective? Isn't it possible that over the years, a particular wheel has developed a bias through constant use? Of course it is. It's not only possible, but probable.

But how does one go about finding a biased wheel? The casino certainly isn't going to hang up a sign over a particular wheel saying "This wheel is out of wack!" On the contrary, the casino inspects each wheel frequently by "skilled technicians" looking for any signs of unusual wear. Dealers must report to the manager whenever they suspect a particular wheel is biased toward a certain segment or side. And it does happen!

To the player's favor, I have serious doubts about the casino's routine inspection. And I'm a little leery of the casino's "skilled technicians." I want to meet one of these guys sometime and see what kind of sophisticated equipment he uses.

Strategy For The "Bias" Player

For the player who is serious about winning, I strongly recommend that you record the activity of a particular wheel before you play. Don't confuse this recommendation with "system" play. You'll be looking for a bias. You'll have sound reasoning for performing your "tests."

If a particular segment of the wheel seems to be getting the most action, by all means play it! But be careful! It could be a bias, but then again, it could be just the unpredictable pattern that occurs from time to time in random numbers. But it might not! And that's the point. Depending on the frequency of your tests . . . and your patience, the results might yield a distinct advantage for you.

Players who are looking for wheel bias can usually be identified by their method of playing a certain segment of the wheel, not a particular number. No bias could be *that* bad. Divide the wheel into approximate quarters or eighths. After you've logged a substantial number of decisions, see if any segment of the wheel is producing more than the natural probabilities for that grouping. Remember, the odds of any one number hitting are 37 to 1. For three numbers, it's 35 to 3; for 8 numbers, it 30 to 8 (15 to 4) and so on.

Looking for wheel bias is no easy task! But it can be fun. And assuming you're not betting the farm while you log all the numbers, it shouldn't cost you one penny. It's the cheapest form of casino entertainment I know of.*

Incidentally, don't expect to measure any bias, if there is any, with only a few minutes of watching. Get serious. Most often, players who are dead-set on finding any bias employ a "team" concept. One member works the wheel for the first hour, the second member for the next hour, and so on. At the end of the period, sometimes days and days, they all gather to compare their data. Of course, there's usually some indication along the way whether or not the effort looks fruitful.

In some cases, casinos have been known to switch wheels on unsuspecting players, and totally destroy all their research. What a crummy deal! If you are beating the wheel through a detected bias, you can expect a

---

*If you are interested in the "wheel bias" concept, I recommend that you read Allan Wilson's *The Casino Gambler's Guide* (Harper & Row), 1970. Wilson devotes a lengthy chapter to this fascinating subject.

His book is one of my favorites. In spite of its copyright date, it remains an excellent value for today's player.

casino countermeasure. The wheel switch is the most common ploy.

THE "WHEEL CLOCKING" ASSAULT

OK, so the idea of standing around a roulette wheel for days on end doesn't excite you. Sure, looking for wheel bias can be downright boring, based on a game that's basically boring anyhow. Only a select few players can really get into it.

But clocking the wheel is a different story. We're not looking for a defect in the wheel, we're looking for a hint as to where the ball will fall, based on three important factors: *the speed of the wheel, the speed of the ball, and the relative position of the ball and the wheel at a particular time.* Does it sound complicated? It really isn't, especially after we analyze it.

Players who believe in clocking a roulette wheel harbor strong feelings about the wheel's inability to produce unpredictable random numbers. Remember, we're not talking about a defect in the wheel itself, but in the design . . . the original concept!

Unlike the keno hopper, where "ping-pong" balls are so thoroughly mixed, and then so randomly selected, the roulette ball might be somewhat predictable based on a calculation of speed and its relationship to the wheel.

Similarly, dice at the craps tables bounce, roll, and rebound with totally unpredictable results. But the only significant "interference" at the roulette wheel that's of any concern to our clocking concept are the few deflectors (canoes) that are placed along the sloping vertical wall to deflect the ball as its momentum decreases.

My personal opinion is that the clockers have a valid argument about the wheel's value as a nonprophetic random number generator. In our final chapter, we'll study the clocking concept in greater detail, giving you my own personal assault (it's not a system) that works along these same lines, but focuses more on the roulette dealer's uncanny and unintentional tendency to spin the ball (and the wheel) at remarkably similar speeds, time and time again.

Since the dealers spin the ball so many times each day and every week, they tend to develop a "programmed" motion, much like we all try to do swinging a golf club, or rolling a bowling ball. Their "delivery" seems to be "grooved," especially if they've been doing it for a long time.

Clocking the wheel, and my way—clocking the dealer, have strong possibilities that we must consider. As I said, we'll devote more to the subject because it's the essence of beating roulette.

ROULETTE NEEDS A NEW TWIST

It's easy to see why the game has deteriorated so much in the last few decades. Without the clocking idea, or even the wheel bias concept, and even the systems we talked about earlier, roulette is not only boring but so totally predictable. Predictable indeed! You can correctly predict that you will lose over the long term . . . and it doesn't have to be that long with a healthy 5.26% going against you on every spin.

Roulette has lost much of its appeal because the house advantage is too steep for the great majority of today's sophisticated and discriminating players who simply know better. It's so much easier to find a better casino game to attack mathematically such as baccarat or craps. Baccarat offers the player a modest 1% house advantage. Better yet, some bets at craps give the casino a tiny ½% edge.

With today's computers, powerful strategies have been performed to aid blackjack players so that the house edge can be virtually eliminated. Of course, these much talked-about strategies only identify the optimum conditions so that the player knows when to increase the size of his bets. Regardless, most of the activity in the casino is at the blackjack tables, and the casinos should be thankful. Only a few players, a very few, can take full advantage.

Times change, and the casino must recognize that their players are changing too. The casino games are certainly not immune. Roulette, without an inside track, is not a good deal.

Devices

A few expert roulette players who are proficient at clocking the wheel have devised elaborate devices built with microprocessors to judge the speed of the ball and the wheel, compute the relationship between the ball and the wheel position, then instantly determine a most likely section of the wheel where the ball will drop.

This sort of ammunition for the player will make roulette more exciting, and give the game a shot in the arm like the computer strategies have done for black-jack. Unfortunately, the casinos are reacting much the same as they did in the 1960's when the new blackjack strategies were revealed. They're fighting back.

In 1985, Nevada Governor Richard Bryan signed into law a bill that makes it unlawful for any person to use or possess any device to assist in projecting the outcome of a game. So much for clocking a roulette wheel right? Well, not really. Only "devices" are outlawed. We can still use our brains. I still think there's a way to legally and ethically clock the wheel, using the device between our ears. And we'll get to that in more detail in our final chapter.

Indeed, roulette needs a new twist to make it interesting. Hopefully, I've wetted your appetite. But before we can get to a serious discussion about wheel-clocking, we must learn more about the game itself: the rules, the wagers, and the payoffs. We have to know as much as possible about the game before we can have any chance at all to beat it.

CHAPTER 2

HOW TO PLAY

For those of you who are not familiar with how roulette is played, a brief review of the game and its rules are in order.

THE WHEEL

The wheel itself has 38 numbered compartments: the numbers 1 through 36, plus two green "numbers," 0 and 00. Eighteen of the numbers are black, and eighteen of the numbers are red. If the green numbers were not on the wheel, the player would have a 50-50 chance (1 to 1 odds) that the ball lands in a black (or in a red) compartment.

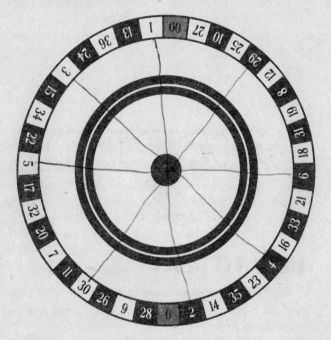

The wheel is carefully laid out so that red and black compartments alternate, except at the green "00" position where both "1" and "27" are otherwise adjacent, and at the green "0" position where both "28" and "2" are otherwise together. More so, a pair of even numbers alternates with a pair of odd numbers, except near the green positions.

The only other "intelligent" aspect of the numbering format is the placing of an odd number on the wheel with the next highest even number directly opposite, and in different colors. For example, "2" is directly opposite "1," and "4" is directly across from "3."

THE BALL

The ball is controlled by the dealer, who propells it around a track at the upper section of the wheel's housing. It's interesting to note that the wheel spins in a counter-clockwise direction, while the ball spins clockwise. The wheel itself weighs over 100 pounds and thereby creates a fly-wheel effect that keeps it spinning at a minimum speed for a surprisingly long period. Furthermore, the wheel is point-balanced for minimum friction. The dealer only occasionally has to give it a boost.

As the ball's speed diminishes, it leaves the track and comes to rest in one of the 38 compartments. Along the way, a series of deflectors in the shape of a "canoe" will catch the ball and help to promote a random result. Some wheels have eight such obstacles, while some of the newer versions have sixteen, equally spaced around the wheel's housing. Deflectors provide the main threat to a wheel-clocker.

Each compartment, all precisely the same size and shape, is formed with metal partitions (called frets) that also tend to deflect the ball as it seeks its final resting spot.

Most players assume the ball is made of precision-machined ivory, and it was until recently. Now, the little white ball is made of precision-machined plastic. Either not enough elephants, or too many pianos.

THE BET

There are eleven different kinds of bets that you can make at a roulette table: a single number; two, three, four, five, six, or twelve-number groups; a column of twelve numbers; the color red or black; whether the number is odd or even; and whether the number is from 1 to 18, or 19 to 36.

Of all these bets, only the single number wager is of interest to the wheel-clocker. Of course, the bet can't be for just any one number; that would be too hard to pin-point. Usually, a wheel-clocker will select a group of six to eight numbers, all adjacent on the wheel, and make a single-number wager on each number.

THE TABLE

The roulette wheel is positioned at the far end of a long table which also includes the betting layout. The dealer stands between the wheel and the betting layout, while up to six players are seated around the area of the table where the betting layout is located.

Many authors suggest that certain seats are better

than others in terms of visibility of the layout and convenience in making the wagers. But wheel-clockers are not interested in *any* seat. They stand. Remember, the wheel-clockers aren't just guessing at the numbers like the other less-fortunate players at the table. They are paying close attention to the wheel, the speed, and the relative position of the ball and the wheel at the time the speeds are computed. Accordingly, they must stand close to the wheel; and then be ready in an instant to reach over the players who might be in their way and place their favored bets.

The rule on making bets at the roulette table is a bit loose, but generally, you are not allowed to bet after the dealer has called "no more bets," at a time when the ball is just about to drop from its track. Some dealers might rush the call a little, and some dealers might let you push the limit.

Unlike the conventional roulette player who usually makes his bets before the ball spins, the wheel-clocker must first watch the wheel and the ball, make a decision, and then place his bet. Most casinos alert roulette dealers to be on the watch for this type of player. If the alleged wheel-clocker is winning consistently, or presents a threat to the casino, the floorman in charge of the pit will keep a constant eye on the player and might harrass him a little. At that time, the smart wheel-clocker calls it a day or visits another casino, aware that his "skill" has been noticed.

ROULETTE CHIPS

Making bets at the roulette table is a bit different from any other casino game. In fact, roulette is the only game where the player does not have his own personal spot to place bets. The layout provides only one area for each bet for all the players. If all bets were made with regular-issue casino chips, you can be assured there would be mass confusion. Even Henry Kissinger couldn't straighten it out.

Accordingly, each player's chips must be distinguishable from the other players, and to do this, the casino provides up to seven different colors of chips—a different color for each player.

When you wish to buy roulette chips, the dealer will ask what denomination you desire for the value of each chip. Until you tell him, the roulette chips have no value whatsoever. Once determined, the dealer will place a "marker" button, showing the correct chip value, on your supply of chips located behind the wheel. In addition, some casinos will place a chip of your color directly on the wheel's rim along with an additional marker button on top, to avoid any later confusion or dispute.

All casinos have minimum chip values and minimum bet sizes, that vary widely from one casino to another. In addition, there are maximum bet limits, usually $500 or less. Today, many casinos use 25 cents as the minimum chip value, and some require a $1 or $2 minimum wager.

In addition, the casino usually wants you to buy at least 20 chips, called a "stack." I can't honestly tell you why, but it's a long-established rule, so go with it. Give the dealer $20 and you'll receive 20 $1 chips, or 40 50-cent chips, whatever value you want them.

Remember, the chips have a value only at the roulette wheel, and only at that time that you're playing. *Never leave the roulette wheel with roulette chips in your pocket.* You'll be stuck if you do. It's an important aspect of the game to always remember.

Incidentally, if the table is not busy (as is usually the case), most dealers won't mind if you wager with regular casino chips, provided no other player is doing the same. And many casinos will let you wager real money, and pay off in casino chips. But always check with the dealer first, to learn the rules in effect at that particular time.

INSIDE AND OUTSIDE BETS

All bets at the roulette wheel are divided into two categories: "inside" and "outside" bets.

Inside bets are made by placing your chip (or stack of chips as one wager) on a single number, or at certain locations on the layout (actually on the lines of the boxes) to signify a group of numbers from two to six.

Any inside bet must meet the table minimum, however the casino will allow multiple bets of less than the table minimum provided they total the table minimum

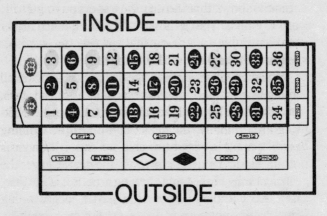

or more. In some casinos, a relatively small maximum wager is posted, such as $25 maximum on inside numbers. The casino's theory on this restricted maximum bet is based on the high payoff odds for inside betting. A player on an incredible win streak could possibly "hurt" the casino with exceptionally large bets. That's the casino's answer. Personally, with such high maximum wagers at the craps tables on the high-odds proposition bets, and at the baccarat tables where maximum limits are often raised to $6,000 or more, I believe it makes little sense to restrict the roulette limits, unless of course, the casino questions the predictability of their own game.

Always check before you play to be sure you understand the betting limits, especially if you're playing in different casinos.

Outside bets are made by placing your chips in the

sections shown that identify the wagers paying 2 to 1, or 1 to 1 odds. The casinos usually allow a much higher maximum bet for the outside wagers, but *each* bet requires at least the table minimum.

When payoffs are made, the dealer first removes all losing wagers. Next, the dealer pays off all outside bets, but leaves the bet (and the payoff) in the respective betting area. Finally, the dealer computes the winning payoffs in the inside betting area and slides the payoffs to the winning player. However, the dealer leaves the original wager in the same betting area. So, it's important that you pick up your chips after each winning bet, unless you wish to press the bet (provided it's under the table maximum), otherwise the bet will indeed work on the next spin, whether you wanted it to or not. Be careful.

For those readers who are not thoroughly familiar with all these bets, it might appear so far that I've done a nice job taking an otherwise simplistic game and making it too damn complicated. Well, the next few pages should help immensely as we look at each individual bet, describe it, and show it to you on the layout. Pay attention.

STRAIGHT-UP BET (ONE NUMBER)

A straight-up bet is simply a bet on a single number. On our sample layout, we've shown a straight-up bet on the numbers 14, 29, and 0. Since there are 38 different compartments on the wheel, there are a total of 38 different straight-up bets that you can make.

Like all bets, the straight-up wager wins or loses on the next spin of the wheel. And, you can wager on as many different numbers as you like.

Be sure that you place your chip completely inside the boxed number. Don't touch a line because that will denote a different type of bet that we'll cover next.

A straight-up bet pays 35 to 1.

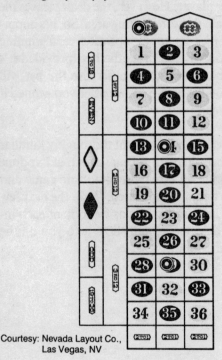

Courtesy: Nevada Layout Co.,
Las Vegas, NV

SPLIT BET (TWO NUMBERS)

A split bet is made by placing your chip on the line, any line, that separates two adjacent numbers on the layout.

A split bet gives you two numbers that are working for you on the next spin of the wheel. If either number hits, you win!

On our illustration, we've indicated three split bets: the numbers 4 and 5; 16 and 19; and 0 and 1.

There are 62 different ways to make a split bet.

A split bet pays 17 to 1.

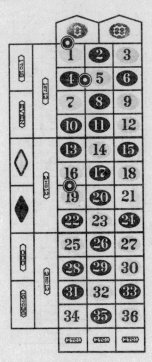

STREET BET (THREE NUMBERS)

A street bet gives you three different numbers with just one wager. The bet is made by placing your chip as shown on our layout, on the line that separates the inside and outside betting area, giving you that particular row of three numbers. In addition, you can make a street bet on the 0-1-2, 0-2-00, and 2-00-3 as shown on our chart.

There are 15 possible combinations of three-number wagers you can make.

A street bet pays 11 to 1.

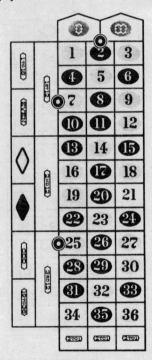

CORNER BET (FOUR NUMBERS)

A corner bet is one of the most popular bets at the roulette table, but don't ask me why.

The chip must be placed at the junction of four numbers. We've indicated two different 4-number bets on the layout: 20-21-23-24; and 1-2-4-5.

There are 22 possible corner bets that you can make.

A corner bet pays 8 to 1 odds.

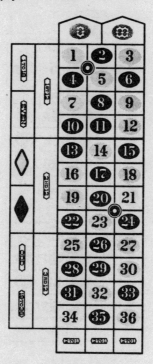

FIVE-NUMBER BET (FIVE NUMBERS)

This bet is the only one that is not recommended, because the house advantage is greater than the game's otherwise consistent 5.26%.

There's no particular reason to make this bet, so let's not spend much time on it. Forget it.

The five-number bet pays 6 to 1.

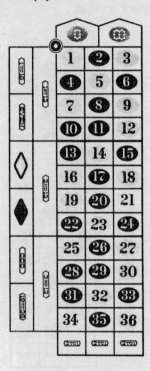

LINE BET (SIX NUMBERS)

Here's a relatively unpopular bet that provides the player with six numbers for a single wager. Think of it as a "double" street bet, where you have two adjacent streets of numbers.

This bet must be placed between two rows of three numbers, on the line at the left of the inside layout.

There are 11 ways to make a six-number line bet.

The line bet pays off at 5 to 1 odds.

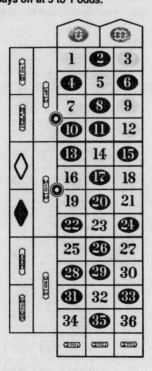

COLUMN BET (TWELVE NUMBERS)

The column bet is an outside wager that allows the player to cover 12 numbers, representing one of the three vertical columns of a dozen numbers.

On our sample illustration, we've shown the column at the far right, beginning with 3 and ending with 36. Most column players prefer this row because the numbers in the column are easy to remember: the common multiples of 3 beginning with 3 . . . 3-6-9-12-15 etc.

There are obviously three different ways to make a column bet. **Column bets pay 2 to 1 odds.**

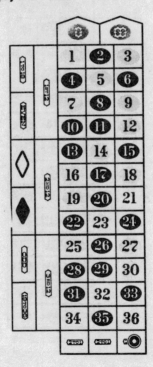

DOZEN BET (TWELVE NUMBERS)

This bet is another way of covering 12 numbers, but unlike the column bet, the numbers are in numerical order: 1 through 12; 13 through 24; and 25 through 36.

Your wager should be placed in the outside section indicating the 1st 12, 2nd 12, or 3rd 12. The dozen bet represents another popular wager that a lot of players prefer.

On our sample layout, we've indicated a dozen bet for the middle third, 13 through 24.

The dozen bet pays 2 to 1 odds.

RED OR BLACK (18 NUMBERS)

This is the bet that most novice players like to make, and for many players is the essence of the game. You have the best likelihood of winning as compared to the inside wagers, but the odds payoff is greatly reduced to even money.

The diamonds at the far left center of the betting layout are in black and red, and indicate the position for making this wager.

A red or black bet pays 1 to 1 odds.

ODD OR EVEN (18 NUMBERS)

This bet is similar to the red or black wager we just described, except you're betting on whether the number that wins is an odd number or an even number. Like red or black, you have only two choices. It can't be that tough.

The boxes for making this bet are easily identified.

An odd or even bet pays 1 to 1 odds.

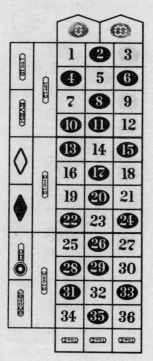

1-18 OR 19-36 BET (18 NUMBERS)

This bet is another even money proposition, whereby you're guessing whether the winning number will be low or high.

Again, the correct box for making the wager is obvious.

Of the three even money wagers, this bet is the least popular.

The 1-18 or 19-36 bet pays 1 to 1 odds.

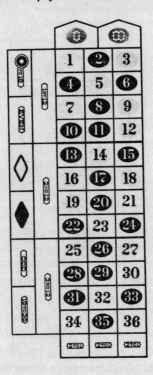

CHAPTER 3

IMPROVING THE ODDS

THE SINGLE ZERO WHEEL

So far in this text, all discussions about roulette have been in reference to the "double zero" wheel with both the green "0" and "00." But some casinos in both Nevada and Atlantic City have experimented from time to time with the "European style" single zero wheel, in the hopes of attracting more players. The single zero wheel has only one green spot, for a total of 37 positions as compared to 38 with the extra "00." **Since the single zero wheel pays off at the same odds as the double zero wheel, the house percentage is effectively reduced to 2.70%!** The player will lose, accord-

ing to the probabilities, one unit out of 37 trials. 1/37
is 2.70%. As you recall, with the double zero wheel,
the player should lose two units out of 38 or 5.26%.
The European single zero wheel is hard to find, but
for the serious roulette player, it's certainly worth the
effort.

As of this writing in August 1985, only a few casinos
in Nevada, very few, offer the more attractive version.
Surprisingly, several casinos in Atlantic City now offer
the single zero wheel, but generally require a much
higher minimum bet. Since casinos are notorious for
changing their rules frequently, it would be of little
value to publish the names of the casinos now offer-
ing the single zero wheel.

ROULETTE IN ATLANTIC CITY

Besides the possibility of finding a single zero wheel,
casinos in Atlantic City offer the roulette player
another big advantage.

If you're playing a double-zero wheel, and betting
on any of the 1 to 1 payoff wagers: red/black,
odd/even, or 1-18/19-36, the casino will only remove
one-half of your bet if the ball lands in a green compartment. This action is termed "surrender." The net
result to the player is one unit in losses over 38 trials,
or a reduced house percentage of 2.63%!

Until recently, Atlantic City casinos offered an option for the player whereby the European "en prison"
rule could be substituted for the ½ bet loss, although
the net result is the same for the player. "En prison"

means that if the ball lands on a green spot, there is no decision on any bets with 1 to 1 payoffs. The player's bet is placed "in prison" until the next spin of the wheel. Then, if the right number hits, the bet is "removed from prison" (but isn't paid). It's then up to the player to either make the bet again, or remove it from the table. In 1980, the Casino Control Commission dropped the "en prison" feature but left the "surrender" option available.

The "en prison" feature or the surrender rule at a single zero game, if available, will greatly reduce the house advantage to a low 1.35% as represented by a net loss factor of ½ unit in 37 trials. In this situation, roulette, even by simple mathematical standards, is an attractive game! But try to find it. In the great majority of cases, you'll be facing two green compartments (double zero wheel) without the benefit of "en prison" or "surrender." Then, we're back to the 5.26% house advantage which can make slot machines look good!

As you might have already guessed, surrender is not presently offered on single zero wheels in Atlantic City, however, there are some indications that it might be considered in the future to perk up the game. Indeed it should!

Many casinos in Europe and other parts of the world continue to offer en prison on their single zero wheels, so we've included the percentages for this feature on the chart that follows on the next page. Remember, either surrender or en prison cuts the house percentage in half for the 1 to 1 bets.

ROULETTE PAYOFF TABLES

TYPE OF WAGER	NUMBERS COVERED	ACTUAL PAYOFF	DOUBLE ZERO		SINGLE ZERO	
			CORRECT ODDS	HOUSE EDGE	CORRECT ODDS	HOUSE EDGE
Straight-Up	1	35:1	37:1	5.26	36:1	2.70
Split	2	17:1	18:1	5.26	17.5:1	2.70
Street	3	11:1	11.7:1	5.26	11.3:1	2.70
Corner	4	8:1	8.5:1	5.26	8.25:1	2.70
Five-Number	5	6:1	6.6:1	7.89	Not Available	
Line	6	5:1	5.3:1	5.26	5.17:1	2.70
Column	12	2:1	2.2:1	5.26	2.1:1	2.70
Dozen	12	2:1	2.2:1	5.26	2.1:1	2.70
Red/Black	18	1:1	1.1:1 (1.05:1)	5.26 (2.63)	1.05:1 (1.03:1)	2.70 (1.35)
Odd/Even	18	1:1	1.1:1 (1.05:1)	5.26 (2.63)	1.05:1 (1.03:1)	2.70 (1.35)
1-18/19-36	18	1:1	1.1:1 (1.05:1)	5.26 (2.63)	1.05:1 (1.03:1)	2.70 (1.35)

The numbers in parentheses represent the odds or house edge for either surrender or en prison that some casinos permit on the 1:1 payoff wagers.

THE MATHEMATICS OF ROULETTE

If the casino pays off your winning wager with an amount that's something less than the true probability of winning that bet, then they have acquired an advantage over you.

As you can see by the chart on the previous page, all wagers are paid off at certain odds that are less than the correct odds of winning.

For example, a split bet pays $17 to a $1 wager, but should pay $18. Remember that the total of both numbers in a correct odds expression represents all the possible outcomes (probabilities). So in the case of our split bet, the total number of probabilities is 19 (18 + 1). To find the house advantage, all we have to do is divide the number of units (dollars, in this case) that we will lose by the total number of probabilities. If the casino pays us $17 but should have paid $18, we are short $1 (our loss). $1 divided by 19 is .0526 or 5.26 cents lost out of each dollar. As a percentage, simply move the decimal two places to the right (just like we did to get cents) and we have 5.26%. That's the casino's advantage, and it applies on each and every spin.

A careful look at our chart shows us that playing the double zero wheel with surrender (in Atlantic City) is almost the same advantage to us as playing a single zero wheel (without surrender). The difference is only .07%!

Confirming that surrender at the double zero wheel

yields 2.63% for the 1:1 payoff bets is easy to do. Again, we know there are 38 total probabilities. 18 of our numbers will win one unit, and 18 numbers will lose one unit. Two numbers (both green) will each lose 1/2 unit. So, in 38 trials, we should lose a total of 1 unit (1/2 + 1/2). 1/38 equals 2.63%.

At the single zero wheel, these same 1:1 payoff bets also gives us one losing unit, but out of only 37 probabilities (37 compartments). And 1/37 equals 2.70%.

Confirming the Odds On Multi-Number Payoffs

The only mathematical part of roulette that many players can't understand relates to the payoff for the split bet and all the other multiple-number inside bets. For example, most players know that the actual payoff for a straight-up bet (one number) is 35 to 1. Since a split bet is for two numbers, it would appear that the correct payoff for a split bet should be half as much as for one number, one-half of 35 to 1, or 17½ to 1. But the casino only pays 17 to 1 for a winning split bet. It looks like the casino has shorted you another one-half unit.

Actually, 17 to 1 is the correct payoff and yields the same house percentage as a straight-up bet because the casino will not take the half of your wager that represents the losing number of your two-number bet.

Confused? OK, let's try it again. If you're making a $2 wager on a split bet of numbers 4 and 7, and number 4 hits, the casino will pay you $34 for your winning number, and leave all of your original bet on the table for you.

Technically, 1/2 of your $2 bet won, and 1/2 lost. But the casino considers the bet as either a win or a loss. If either number hits, it's a win. Since the casino does not take the half of your wager that lost, it makes up for the apparent discrepancy.

A $2 split bet will yield the same payoff as two straight-up bets for $1 each on the same numbers. Remember, your $2 split bet wins $34. If you would have wagered $1 on each of the numbers 4 and 7, you would have won $35 for the winning number 4, and lost the other $1 for the losing number 7. See, you yield a net win of $34 either way. Got it?

WHAT THE CASINOS SAY

Generally, I like to support the information I provide to my readers by surveying casinos for timely and authoritative data, and to confirm my opinions and recommendations. Sometimes, it's necessary to go to the casino commissions that set the rules and enforce the laws in Nevada and Atlantic City. I can think of no better sources.

Single Zero Wheels

There were few casino managers who showed any enthusiasm for roulette; it would appear that the game is somewhat bland from both sides of the table.

In downtown Las Vegas, the El Cortez gets a fair amount of action, according to 11-year shift boss, Wayne Starker. He indicated to me that the casino had experimented with single zero wheels from time to time, but returned to the double zero game because the "new" game didn't get much more action. If you recall from our previous discussions, the single zero wheel cuts the house percentage from 5.26% to 2.70%. But not enough players appreciated the change. Starker thinks that a lot of players didn't realize the difference in the percentages, and for that matter, might not have even realized that the wheels were any different at all!

This same account had been related to me by several other casino managers which certainly doesn't say very much for roulette players. According to Paul Burst, director of casino operations for the Claridge Hotel in Atlantic City, they too tried the single zero wheel and soon realized that ". . . the action was pretty much the same. The small increase in the drop was not enough to justify the lower hold." Incidentally, the term "drop" means all the cash and credit slips that are dropped into the slot of the table and into a metal holding bin. The "hold" represents the casino's percentage; a more literal term for the money the casino makes as their advantage in all the games.

At the Sands in Las Vegas, casino manager Doug DuCharme can recall a single zero wheel when he first started there a few years ago. Of course, the wheel is long gone, and you can pretty much guess why.

Some of the hotels I talked to that do offer the single zero wheel, generally require a higher minimum bet. Instead of a dollar or two, the minimum bet might be as high as $25. So, either the player doesn't know what he's looking for, or does . . . but when he finds it, he can't afford it!

Clocking The Wheel

Regarding wheel-clockers, Starker told me that he sees players at the El Cortez with stop-watches and calculators quite frequently. But according to a guy who should know, he says they lose at the same rate as anyone else. As a lot of casino managers told me, "gadgets" at the roulette wheel are commonplace.

Atlantic City has a law much like Nevada that prohibits a player from using an electronic or mechanical device such as a calculator or computer that assists in projecting the outcome of a game, or analyzing the changing probabilities or playing strategies at any table game.

Some casino managers appeared to be sensitive about "devices" and some indicated that they were only mildly concerned.

Much of the concern is at the blackjack tables and directed primarily to card-counters. In the case of roulette, as based on my findings, it would appear you could drag in a mainframe computer, plug in some strobe lights, send the data to NASA, and hold an MIT seminar at the same time . . . without raising an eyebrow.

Well, maybe not. Don't take me serious. Devices are risky, and regardless of some casino's liberal policy, are blatantly unethical.

Past-Posting

In talking with the casino managers, there was no question where they draw the line. Past-posting! This is the most common cheating scam at the roulette tables, and one of the casino's biggest sources of aggravation. A cheater will cleverly sneak a bet on the layout *after* the ball has dropped in a pocket. Sure, it's a great way to pick winners, and it's a great reason to need an attorney. The casinos will prosecute!

According to DuCharme at the Sands, past-posters usually work in teams; one or two members will distract the dealer, while another member actually places the bet. Most often, past-posting is on straight-up bets where the payoffs are 35 to 1. In a short time, the casino can suffer large losses. DuCharme says that on weekends, or whenever busy, it's the practice of most casinos to employ a "mucker," another dealer who stands at the far end of the table and watches only the layout. Otherwise, it's difficult for a single dealer to spot a past-poster with all the action from so many players.

Clocking The Dealer

Besides clocking the wheel, I asked about the little known tactic of clocking the dealer—looking for identical, systematic patterns in the way the dealer spins the wheel and the ball.

DuCharme was quick to point out that his dealers are always instructed to vary the speed and the number of rotations to prevent any possibility of making the outcome predictable.

Interestingly enough, he said that some dealers do indeed begin the spin of the ball, and let go of the ball at almost precisely the same spots on the wheel-head, and over a period of time will actually wear a groove in the track. To counter this, most casinos will rotate the wheel-head a few inches each week or so, to prevent a groove from forming.

More so, some dealers aware of the system, will purposely let their fingers brush the wheel as they spin the ball, thereby slowing the wheel ever so slightly, but enough to throw off the clocker.

"29" THE HARD WAY

Now, let me tell you why wheel-clockers, or dealer-clockers spend the effort. Let me tell you a little story that should shed some new light on this whole discussion.

One of my friends in the casino industry, Russell Scott, casino manager at the Desert Inn in Las Vegas, offered to help us with the photography for the front cover of this book. He said if we were going to use a picture of a roulette wheel on the cover, we should come out and see a particular wheel he had in mind.

The Desert Inn has three roulette wheels in the casino. Two of the wheels are like all the others; relatively new, made with lots of plastic, and not particularly impressive. But one special wheel really stood out. Unlike the others, this one had a picturesque motif along the outside edge, hand-crafted in solid hardwoods. The wheel itself was hand-carved in solid Maple, piece by piece, to form the precise shape and balance of what was more than just a roulette wheel, but a fine work of art.

Scott told me that the wheel, and four others just like it (but now unaccounted for) were commissioned by Wilbur Clark, who in 1950 built the original Desert Inn. The wheel has been in the same casino for over 35 years. God only knows how many spins, how many cheers, and how many lost fortunes. The wheel has a unique character that's difficult to describe. The next time you're at the DI, look for it.

Anyhow, my photographer was busy setting up the shot while an attendant at the casino was cleaning and polishing the wheel for its portrait. As a last thought, I remembered that I wanted to have the ball placed in "29," because it's my son's favorite number. So, I told Scott to put the ball in 29 for me. He said, "You want 29, right?" "Sure," I said, noting that Scott had begun spinning the wheel.

"Now watch closely," he said, as we gathered around wondering what the hell was going on. Scott spun the ball around the track like any dealer does, making the usual ten to twelve revolutions. Were we supposed to believe that the ball would fall in 29? Seriously!

The ball slowed from its track and dropped to the wheel's floor, bounced against the frets that separate the compartments, and to our amazement, landed in 29 black! We couldn't believe it! The attendant began laughing like it was some trick. Scott started laughing; we were all laughing and drawing the attention of others in the casino who were probably wondering what could be so exciting at a closed roulette table.

I immediately checked under the table, like a jerk. Obviously, there was nothing there; no buttons, no switches, no magnets. It was indeed a real roulette wheel in a totally honest casino, not some grind-joint. I was embarrassed that I even looked.

For the rest of the trip, we all pestered Scott with "How did you do that! How did you do that!" His answer was always the same. "Just lucky, that's all . . . just lucky."

CAN A ROULETTE DEALER AFFECT THE OUTCOME?

That's a good question! Can certain experienced dealers really influence the drop of the ball? Was Scott just lucky?

Personally, in the case of that memorable incident at the Desert Inn, yes, I think he was just plain lucky. I have serious doubts that any roulette dealer, or casino boss, could be that precise in exerting any possible influence.

But let's look at this as a matter of degree. We can safely assume that no dealer can make the ball drop in a specific compartment without some sort of trickery. That degree of legitimate skill would be virtually impossible, based on, at the very least, the many deflectors that guard the wheel and catch the ball. I didn't just fall off the onion truck and neither did you.

But isn't it possible that at least some control can be gained, such as 5% or even 10% effectiveness in pinpointing a "section" of the wheel where the ball might drop?

I'm not suggesting that a roulette dealer will cheat the player. Not at all! I'm suggesting that some dealers might be able to predict an outcome based on their many years of acquiring a "feel" for the speed of the ball, and the speed of the wheel.

Significance To The Player

What significance does this mean to the player you ask? Well, any value to the dealers of their own ability is academic. The dealers can't spin the ball and then bet on their own spin. But the players can! It's possible that the dealer's consistent routine in spinning the ball and wheel might occur with astonishing regularity, perhaps unbeknownst to the dealer, and the player who's sharp enough to look for it can base his bets on this perfected routine.

The essence of timing a dealer is to determine if there is any pattern to the spot on the wheel where the ball is released, and the spot where the ball lands.

As you can see, our concern is not predictability on the part of the dealers, but predictability *from the player's standpoint*, based on the likelihood that the dealer is following a strict routine from which both might be able to predict, but only the player can act!

What we are talking about is an acquired ability, no matter how slight and no matter how useless to the dealer. An ability that the dealer has fashioned through trials and trials and trials. A technique not of his own choosing, but as a function of his daily routine.

If you continually hit golf balls eight hours a day, five days a week, chances are you'll eventually be ready for the tour! It's the same thing here. But of course the roulette dealer can't really "use" his technique for any personal gain, at least not in *today's* casinos. I've always believed that 99.99% of all casinos today run honest games. And I've never had any reason to doubt that belief.

Reading The Dealer's Mind

If you're still not convinced that some experienced roulette dealers can develop a predictable routine (not for *their* value, but for *yours*!), put yourself in their position. You've been working the wheel for years and years. After a while, isn't it likely that you would begin to wonder if you could skillfully control the outcome? Isn't it likely that you would eventually decide to "test" your skill during the course of your long work-day? After all, you're being paid to spin the ball, so you might as well have some fun with it.

Eventually, isn't it possible that you might develop an automatic "delivery," no different than the professional golfer's "automatic swing"? A precise, rhythmic style that might lend some predictability to the game?

Surprisingly, a few dealers I talked to confirmed this notion. In fact, one dealer was quite bold in bragging about his "touch."

Remember, I'm not suggesting that any dealer has developed a skill to cheat you. In fact, I was told about a dealer who would occasionally feel sorry for a particular player and would try to help the player win! I'm not sure what it took to qualify for the "help," other than (a) you were losing badly, (b) you reminded him of his mother, or (c) you reminded him of Bo Derek.

I'm not a roulette dealer, so I can't tell you what goes through their minds, and I can't tell you in fact that a skill can be developed. Allowing plenty of room for exaggeration, who's to say that a dealer with a lot of years under his belt can't provide at least a little influence? Who's to say that a dealer has never fell victim to his good Samaritan values? And who's to say what might happen if you walk up to the table with a big, black, smelly cigar?

Keeping The Game Honest

As you can appreciate, any dealer caught trying to help a player win (or lose), would be fired on the spot, although it would be difficult to prove. This brings to mind the possibility that a skilled roulette dealer could indeed line his own pockets by working in collusion with a player as his partner and splitting the profits.

And that gets us back to what we talked about earlier, the importance of the floormen, pit bosses, and casino managers who must insure the honesty of all the games from both sides of the tables.

Russ Scott, for example, has been in the casino business over 40 years. He's seen it all. Part of running a first-class casino like the Desert Inn is to know what *can* happen, what dealers *can* do, and what players *can* do, but shouldn't. And to make sure that indeed it *doesn't* happen, an expert like Scott is the best protection.

He told me how many times a casino is cheated, not only by the players, but by the casino's own dealers —their own employees! To find them, and catch them, you have to know what you're looking for.

There are stories about crooked roulette dealers in illegal joints in the old days who could make the ball drop in a narrow section of the wheel where the house had no action or at least the smallest bets. If a big wager was made on 11, the ball would drop on the opposite side of the wheel. *The dealer had the touch.*

Perhaps the best example in the casino today is the "Big-6" wheel where some dealers have been spinning the thing for decades. They can hit any number blindfolded. I'm not saying they do, I'm saying they can. After all, they've had years and years to practice.

Today, in the major casinos like the Desert Inn, this kind of thing is an inconceivable enemy. The casino's license on the wall is too valuable to risk. The big cheating scams are *against the casino*, and that's what the sharp casino managers are looking for. To protect the casino, *and* to protect the player.

But the real point to this discussion should be obvious. If it's indeed possible that certain experienced dealers can affect the outcome by their "skill," doesn't that also suggest that a player could also develop a skill by measuring these same parameters that lead to the same result? Predictability.

Think about it.

RATING YOUR OPTIONS

Here's what we know.

If you're going to try to beat the roulette wheel with a number system or a betting system, with any consistency, forget it. You have no chance!

If you're going to spend lots of time looking for a wheel bias, and if you're lucky enough to find it, the casino will probably change the wheel. That idea certainly has its drawbacks. But it's interesting.

If you're thinking about a hidden computer, complete with all the neat little attachments to clock the wheel, think again. Remember, the device is illegal.

The only possible edge for the player that might work is to consider clocking the dealer. And I have no quarrels with the ethical issue. Otherwise, we wouldn't even be discussing it. There's no device, and obviously no cheating. It's a function of skill and patience . . . and good eyesight.

There's no point in trying to clock a young, or inexperienced dealer. Repetition is the key here. Lots and lots of spins under the belt; years and years of "practice." Sometimes, I'll ask a dealer how long he has been dealing roulette. The longer the better . . . to develop a constant rhythm.

Remember, *the basis of clocking a dealer is to find out if there is any relationship between the spot on the wheel where the ball is released, and the compartment in which the ball falls*.

If you notice that in eight out of ten times, the ball came to rest in a section of the wheel that's directly opposite the release area, that would certainly seem to indicate a possible pattern. Perhaps the ball came to rest near the same release area. That's fine. There's your section to use.

As you can appreciate, the clocker only bets a section of the wheel, making straight-up bets, usually six to eight numbers that are all adjacent on the wheel.

If you're concerned about the highly remote chance

that a dealer will try to beat you with his "skill," don't worry about it. Remember, you always place your bet *after* the ball has left his hand!

And that reminds me, try to make your bet as soon as possible. Don't push the limits to the point where the ball is bouncing in the pockets. The dealer might think you're trying to past-post the game!

There Are No Guarantees

You must understand that wheel clocking is not an entirely easy affair. There are many snags that you should be aware of. For example, subtle variations in the wheel's speed (or the ball's speed) will make mental wheel clocking totally useless. Although the dealer might be aware of these changes, the player will have great difficulty in detecting them. The best chance for the player is to clock a dealer who is unaware of your attempts, and unaware for that moment of his natural perfection.

It's likely that if the dealer knows you're trying to clock him, he'll purposely vary the speed of either the ball or the wheel to beat you at his own game. After all, the dealer has complete control over the parameters that you're trying to measure. Don't let him know that you're making the effort.

If you walk up to a roulette table, stand around for an hour or so with your nose two feet from the wheel, making notes on a scratch pad while jotting down numbers from your hand-held copy of the roulette wheel numbers, my guess is it'll look a little fishy.

The slick wheel clockers, whoever these people are, have enough skill and knowledge to actually sit at the table (far left side), watch the ball release, and then mentally determine the relationship to the winning compartment *in degrees*, such as 90° or 270°. After a few spins, if they see any consistency, they'll make a few straight-up bets on the numbers that fall into this same sector, but not by looking at their chart of numbers. That's a give-away. They have the numbers on the wheel *memorized*. And that's not easy!

If you're detected trying to clock the wheel, the floorman will probably keep an eye on you. If you show that you're losing like everyone else, he'll no doubt chuckle a little and walk away. But if you're winning, whether your strategy is working or you're just plain lucky, you'll get some pressure. Either the floorman will instruct the dealer to rush the timeframe in which you can make your wagers, or the dealer will be told to greatly vary the speeds.

At that stage, you might as well sit down, relax, and guess at the numbers like everyone else. Or better yet, try a different game.

I've spent a lot of time on wheel clocking because, quite frankly, it's the only interesting part of the game. The game itself is boring as hell. If that's what it takes to generate a little excitement, why not?

Understand that if you're betting on red/black, odd/even, or low/high numbers, the clocking idea has no value. Obviously, with red and black alternating with each compartment, such bets are strictly a guessing game.

But more importantly, I want you to know that these discussions about wheel clocking have been included in this text simply because it's a part of roulette, and has been for many years. This *is* a book about roulette. Without a mention of clocking, the book would be incomplete.

These discussions are not to give you false hope, or any wild ideas about owning your own casino! No matter what you might think, there are no guarantees at the roulette table or at any other casino game, regardless of your skills, your memory, or your determination. Like all the games, I suggest you play only for fun, if indeed you decide to play at all. The concept of wheel clocking is something you might want to consider as you make the small table-minimum bets; something that might add to your enjoyment of the game.

At the very least, we can hope that any effort to time the dealer's spin will help to minimize the casino's built-in advantage. But whether your timing efforts work or not, it always pays to shop for a single zero wheel.

Roulette, in spite of its sagging appeal, is fun to play, especially when you have a full understanding of the game. It helps a great deal if you remember to manage your money wisely, in the most conservative fashion. Never keep playing if you're losing; and always try to quit when you're ahead.

Remember what you're up against . . . over 200 years of profit for casinos all over the world.

Can you beat the game?

I hope you can!

Good luck!